HAL•LEONARD® BASS PLAY-ALONG

AUDIO ACCESS INCLUDED

VOL. 6

CLASSIC ROCK

PLAYBACK+

Speed • Pitch • Balance • Loop

To access audio, visit:
www.halleonard.com/mylibrary

Enter Code
1374-2648-6943-1973

ISBN 978-0-634-09004-2

HAL•LEONARD®

Visit Hal Leonard Online at
www.halleonard.com

Contact us:
Hal Leonard
7777 West Bluemound Road
Milwaukee, WI 53213
Email: info@halleonard.com

In Europe, contact:
Hal Leonard Europe Limited
42 Wigmore Street
Marylebone, London, W1U 2RN
Email: info@halleonardeurope.com

In Australia, contact:
Hal Leonard Australia Pty. Ltd.
4 Lentara Court
Cheltenham, Victoria, 3192 Australia
Email: info@halleonard.com.au

contents

Free Ride

Words and Music by Dan Hartman

Intro
Moderately fast ♩ = 128

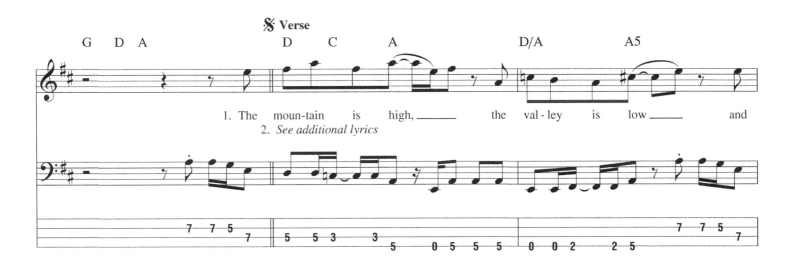

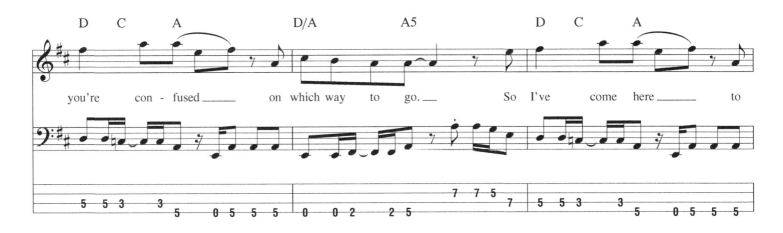

1. The moun-tain is high, _____ the val-ley is low _____ and
2. *See additional lyrics*

you're con - fused _____ on which way to go. _____ So I've come here _____ to

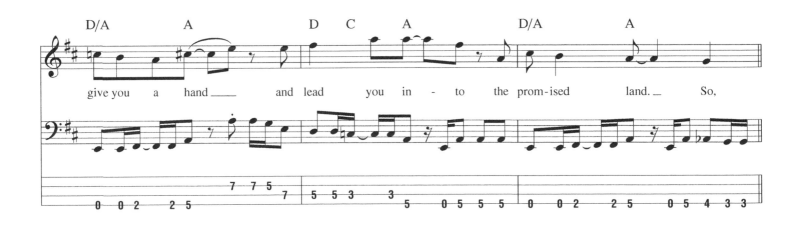

give you a hand _____ and lead you in - to the prom-ised land. _____ So,

Chorus

come on _____ and take a free ride. _ Come on _____ and stand here

To Coda ⊕

by my side. _____ Come on _____ and take a free ride.

D.S. al Coda

|1., 2., 3. | |4.|

Guitar Solo

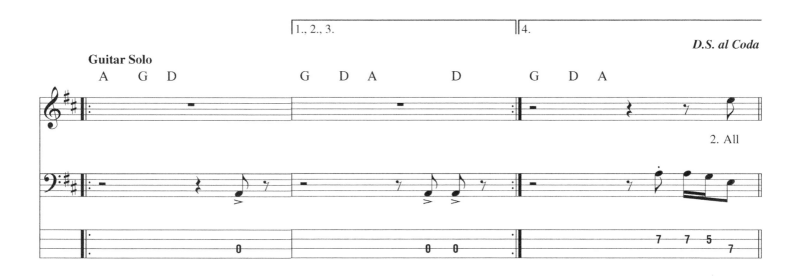

2. All

⊕ **Coda**

Yeah,   yeah,   yeah, yeah.

1., 2., 3.

4.

Begin fade

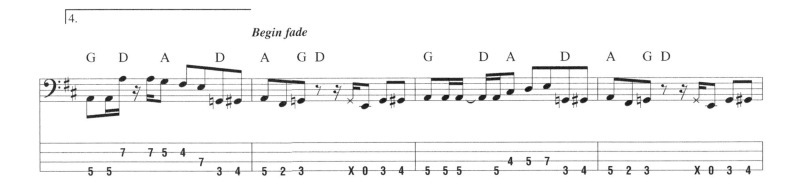

Fade out

Additional Lyrics

2. All over the country I've seen it the same,
   Nobody's winning at this kind of game.
   We've gotta do better, it's time to begin.
   You know all the answers must come from within.

Gimme Three Steps

Words and Music by Allen Collins and Ronnie Van Zant

Intro
Moderate Rock ♩ = 132

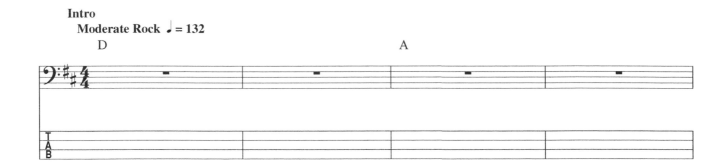

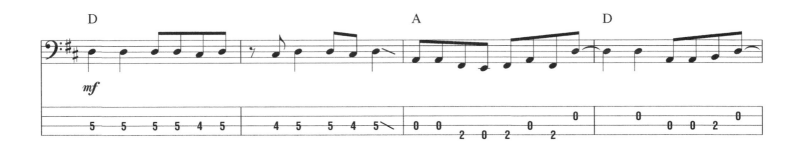

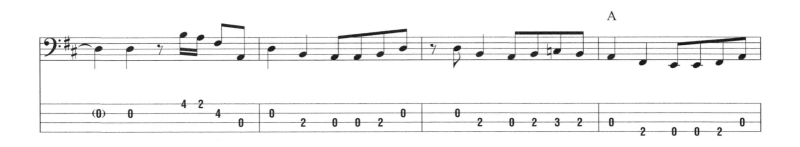

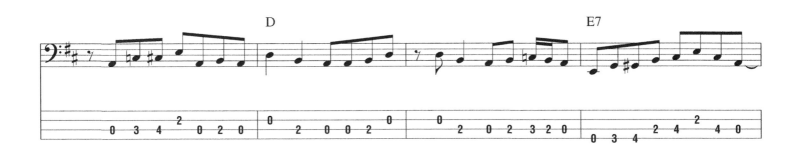

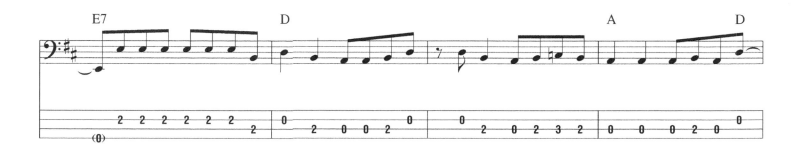

Verse

1. I was cut - tin' the rug ___ down at a place called The Jug ___ with a girl named ___ Lin - da Lu ___ when ___

in walked a man ___ with a gun in his hand ___ and he was look-ing for you know who. ___

He said, "Hey___ there fel - low with the hair col - ored yel - low,

what you try - in' to prove? ___   'Cause that's   my wom - an there ___ and I'm a

man who ___ cares ___ and this   might be ___ all   for you." ___

Guitar Solo

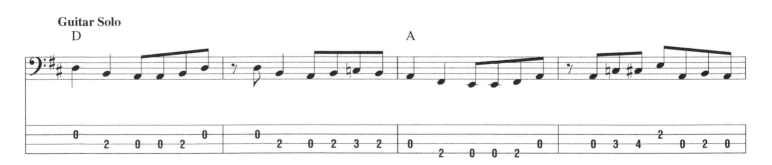

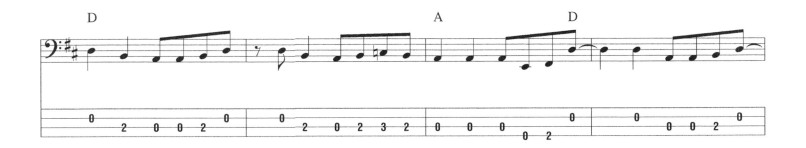

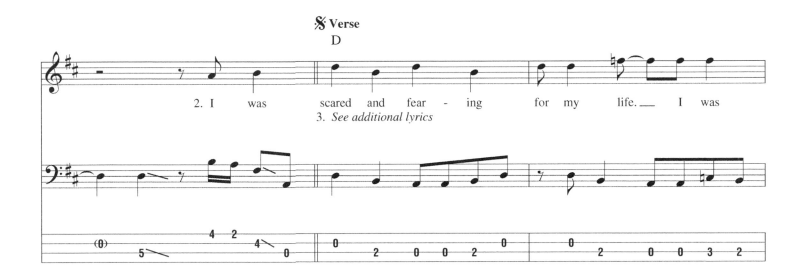

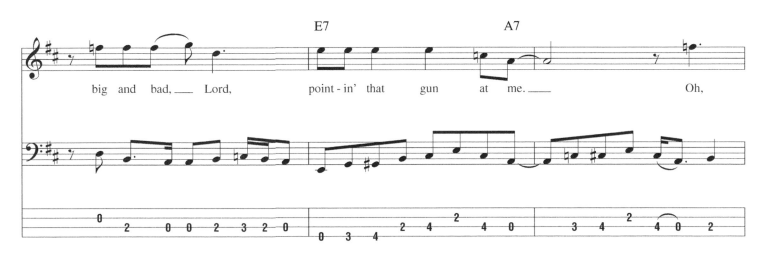

wait a min-ute, mis-ter. I did-n't e-ven kiss her. Don't want no trou-ble with you.___

___ And I know ___ you don't owe me but I wish you would let ___ me

2nd time, substitute Fill 1

ask one fa-vor from you. ___ Oh, won't you

Fill 1

gim-me three steps, gim-me three steps, mis - ter. Gim-me three steps to-ward the door._

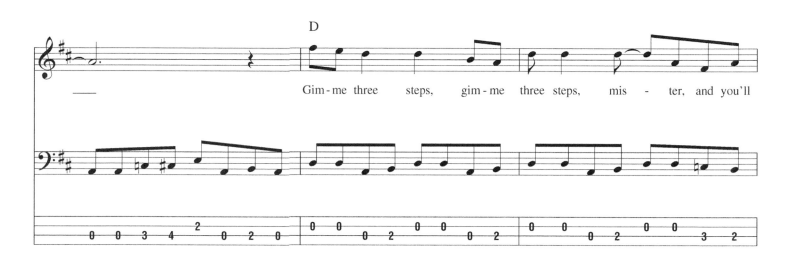

_ Gim-me three steps, gim-me three steps, mis - ter, and you'll

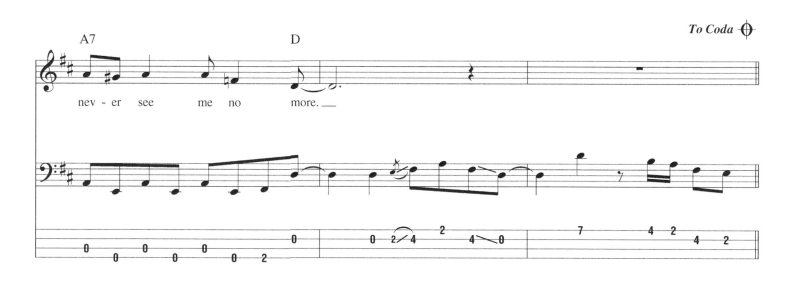

To Coda ⊕

nev - er see me no more. __

Guitar Solo

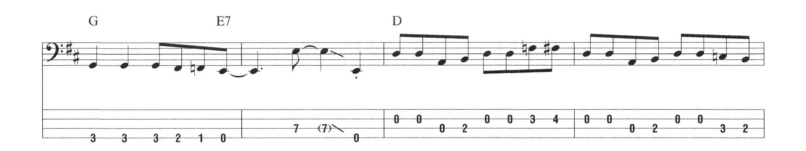

D.S. al Coda

Coda

Outro-Guitar Solo

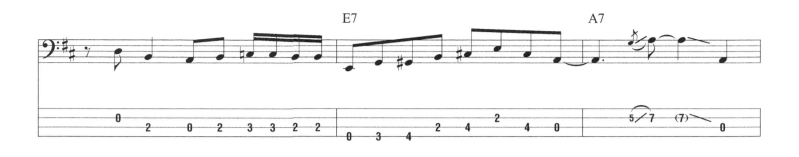

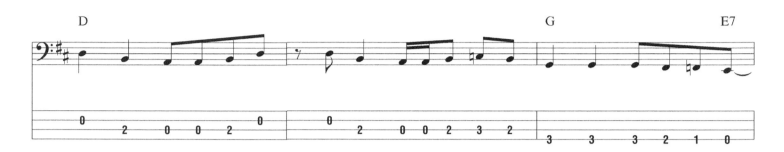

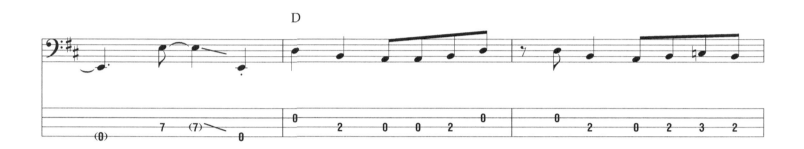

Begin fade

Fade out

Additional Lyrics

3. Well, the crowd cleared away and I began to pray
And the water fell on the floor.
And I'm tellin' you, son, well, it ain't no fun
Starin' straight down a forty-four.
Well, he turned and screamed at Linda Lu
And that's the break I was lookin' for.
And you could hear me screamin' a mile away
As I was headin' out t'wards the door.

Funk #49

Words and Music by Joe Walsh, Dale Peters and James Fox

Intro
Moderate Rock ♩ = 92

1. A -

Verse

sleep all day, ___ out all night, ___ I know where you're go - in'.

I don't think ___ that's act - in' right, ___ you don't think it's show - in'.

Interlude

jump-in' up, fall - in' down, __ don't mis - un - der - stand me.

3. See additional lyrics

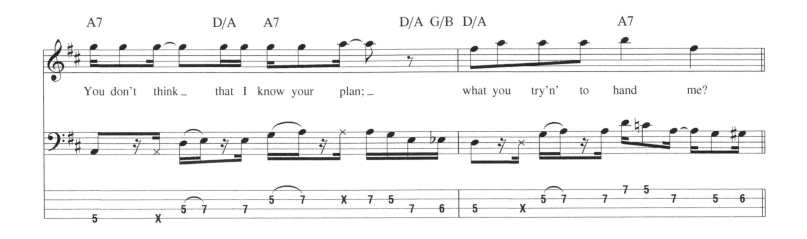

You don't think _ that I know your plan; _ what you try'n' to hand me?

Interlude

To Coda ⊕

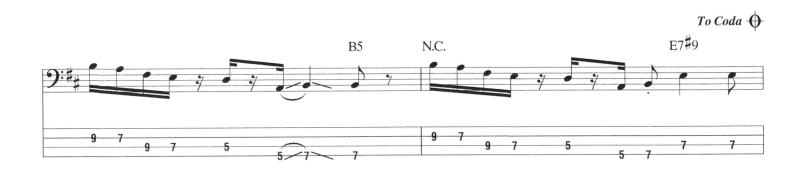

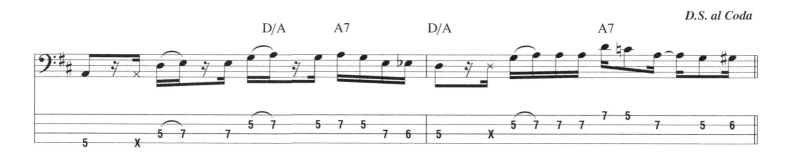

Begin fade

Fade out

Additional Lyrics

3. Out all night, sleep all day,
   I know what you're doin'.
   If you're gonna act this way,
   I think there's trouble brewin'.

Green-Eyed Lady

Words and Music by Jerry Corbetta, J.C. Phillips and David Riordan

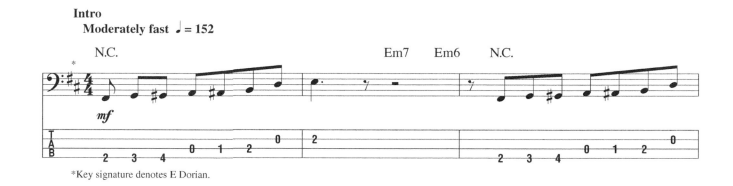

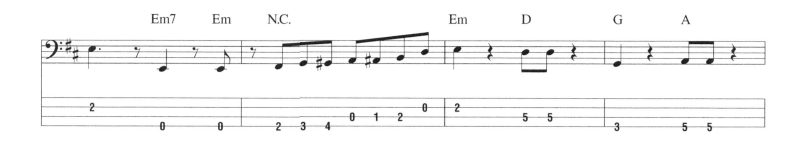

*Key signature denotes E Dorian.

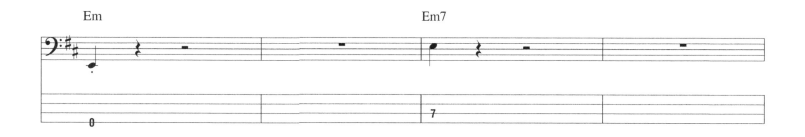

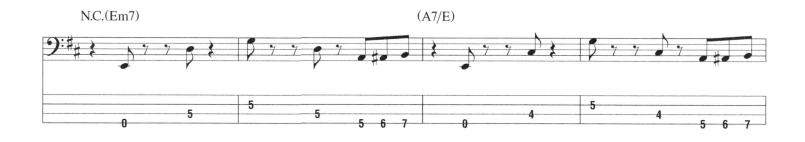

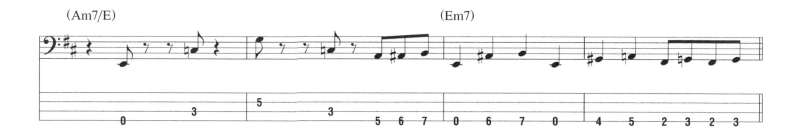

% Verse

1. Green-eyed la - dy, love-ly la - dy. ___ Stroll - ing
2. *See additional lyrics*

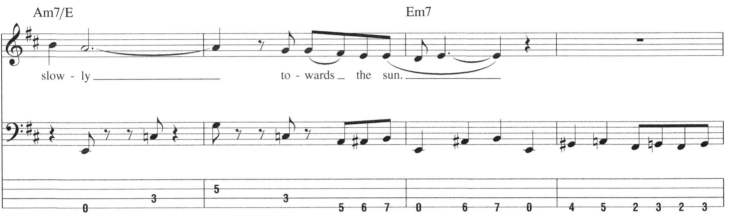

slow - ly _____ to - wards ___ the sun. ___

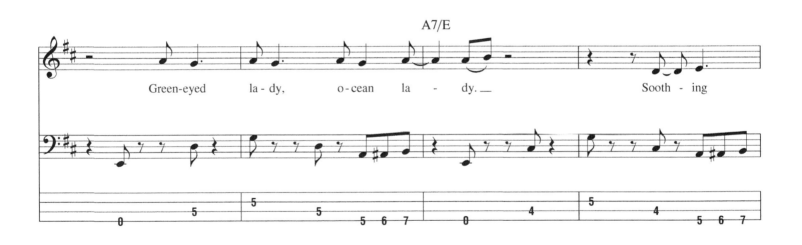

Green-eyed la - dy, o - cean la - dy. ___ Sooth - ing

ev - 'ry ___ rag - ing wave ___ that comes. ___

To Coda

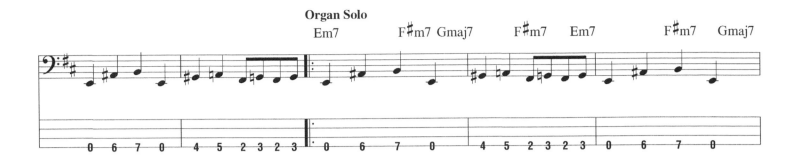

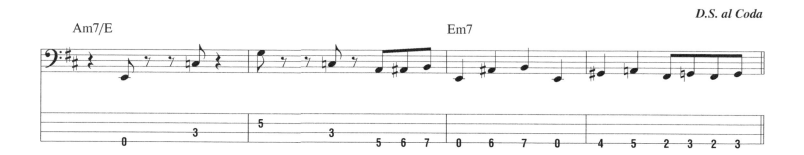

Additional Lyrics

2. Green-eyed lady, wind-swept Lady.
   Rules the night, the waves, the sand.
   Green-eyed lady, ocean lady.
   Child of nature, friend of man.
   Green-eyed lady, passions lady.
   Dressed in love, she lives for life to be.
   Green-eyed lady feels life,
   I never see setting suns and lovely lovers free.

Radar Love

Words and Music by George Kooymans and Barry Hay

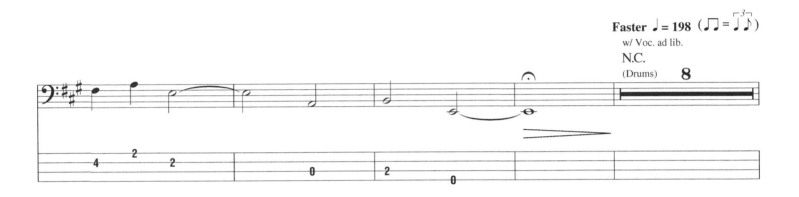

Pre-Chorus

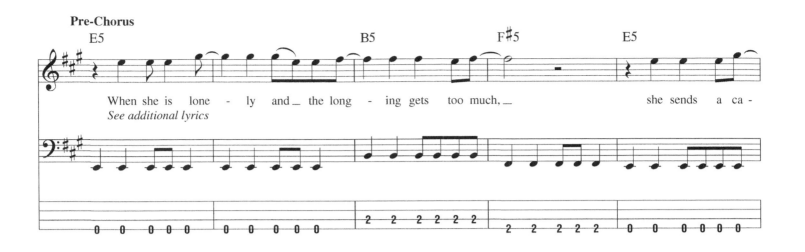

When she is lone - ly and the long - ing gets too much, she sends a ca-
See additional lyrics

- ble com - ing in from a - bove. Don't need a phone at all.

Chorus

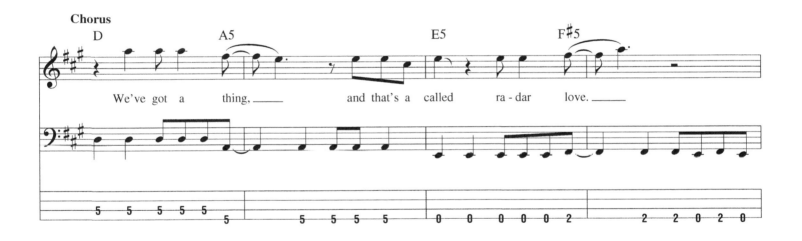

We've got a thing, and that's a called ra - dar love.

To Coda

We've got a wave in the air.
We've got a light in the sky.

Ra - dar

Interlude

N.C.(F#m7)

love.

1., 2.   3.

D.S. al Coda

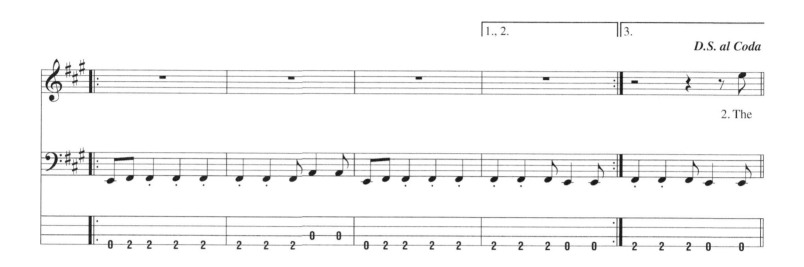

2. The

Coda

Interlude

N.C.(F#m7)   F#m7

Play 8 times

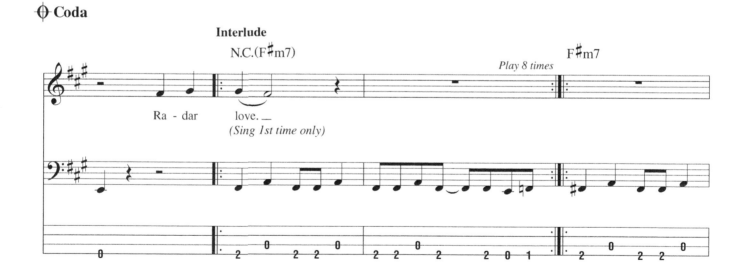

Ra - dar   love.

(Sing 1st time only)

C#5

Play 24 times

Breakdown
N.C.
(Drums)

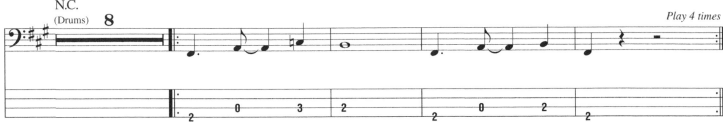

E5

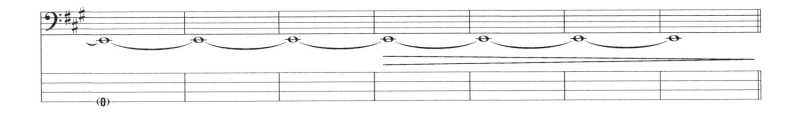

Interlude
N.C.(F#m7)

ra - di - o played _ that for - got - ten song. _

Bren - da Lee, _ it's com - in' on strong. _____ And the

news man sang his ___ same song. _ Oh, _

one more ra - dar lov - er gone. _____

Pre-Chorus

When I ___ get lone - ly and I'm sure I've had e - nough, ___ she sends a com -

- fort com - ing in ___ from a - bove. ___ We don't need no let-ter at all. ___

Chorus

We've ___ got a thing ___ that's called ___ ra - dar love. ___

We've ___ got a light ___ in the sky. ___

We've ___ got a thing _____ that's called a ra - dar love. ___

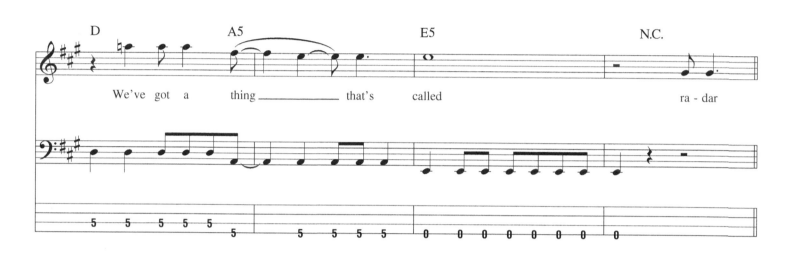

We've got a thing _____ that's called ra - dar

Interlude

N.C.(F#m)

love. ___
(Sing 1st time only)

Outro

F#m7

Play 3 times

Play 5 times

Additional Lyrics

2. The radio's playin' some forgotten song.
   Brenda Lee comin' on strong.
   The road has got me hypnotized,
   And I'm spinnin' into a new sunrise.

Pre-Chorus   When I get lonely and I'm sure I've had enough,
   She sends a comfort coming in from above.
   We don't need no letter at all.

White Room

Words and Music by Jack Bruce and Pete Brown

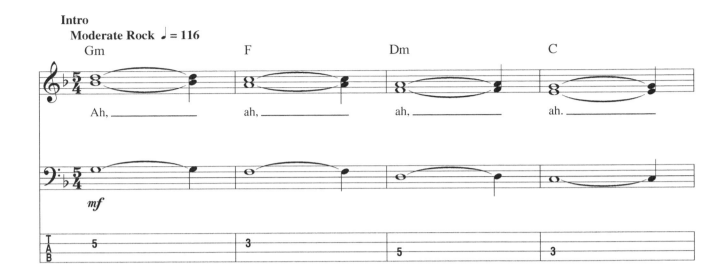

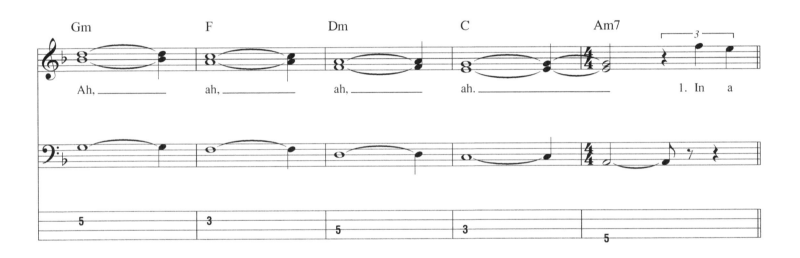

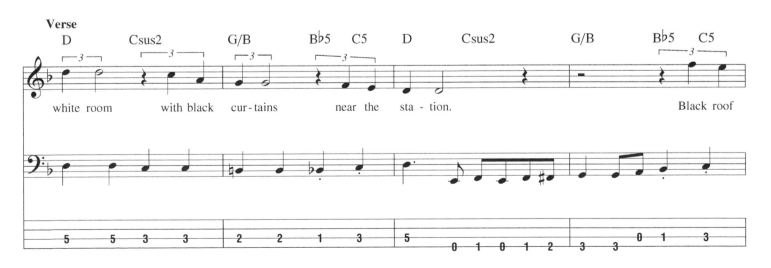

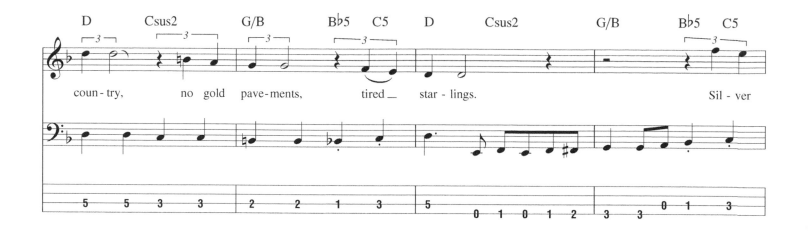

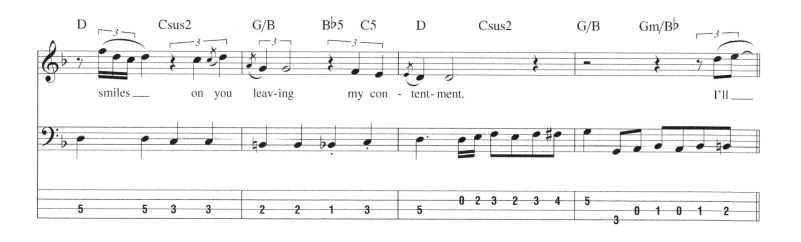

Bridge

place where the shad - ows run _____ from them - selves. 2. You said

Verse

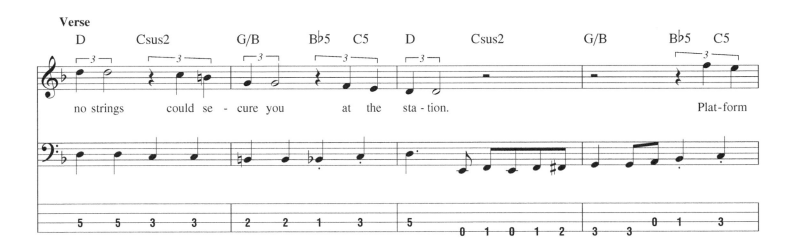

no strings could se - cure you at the sta - tion. Plat-form

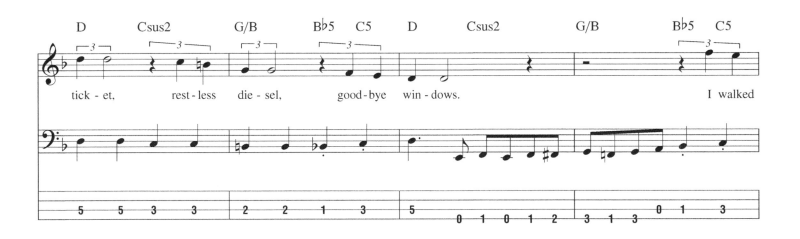

tick - et, rest - less die - sel, good - bye win - dows. I walked

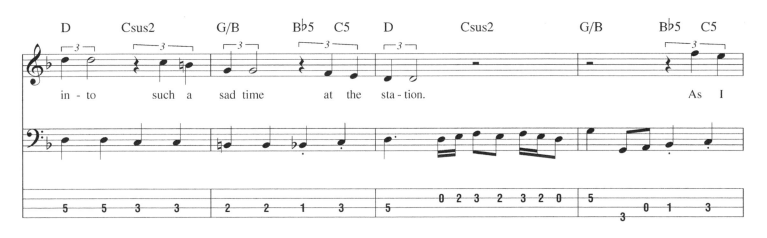

in - to such a sad time at the sta - tion. As I

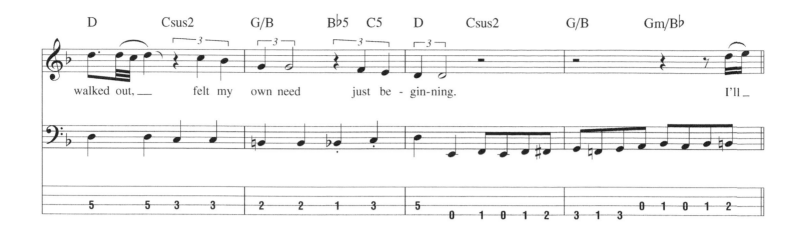

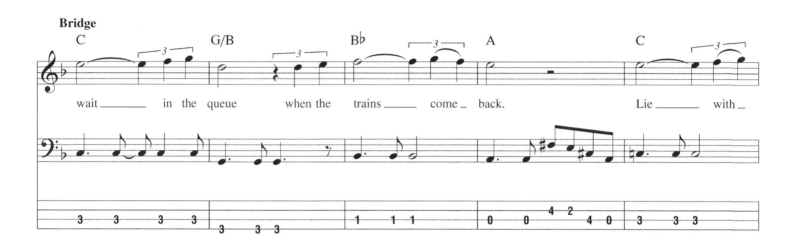

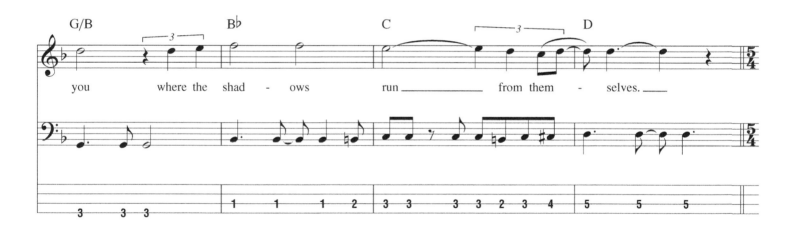

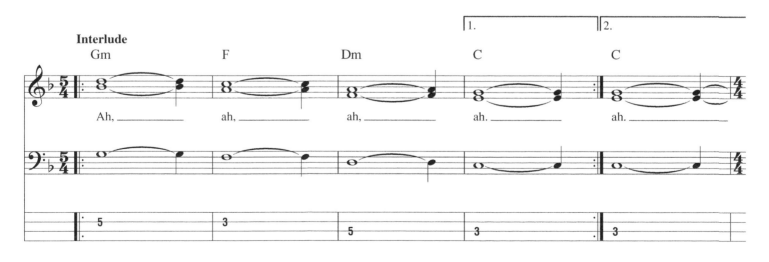

Verse

3. At the par-ty she was kind-ness in the hard crowd.

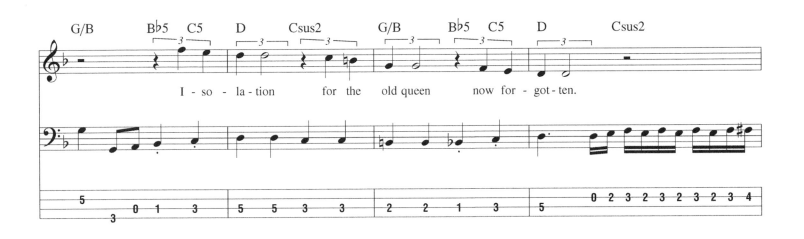

I - so - la - tion for the old queen now for - got - ten.

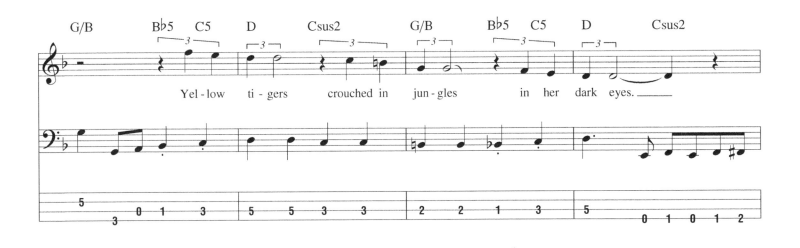

Yel - low ti - gers crouched in jun - gles in her dark eyes.

She's just dress-ing good-bye win-dows, tired star - ling.

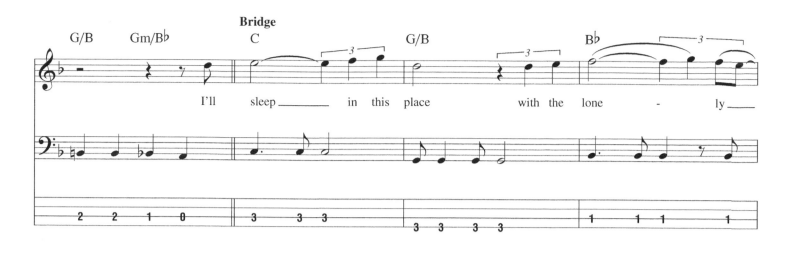

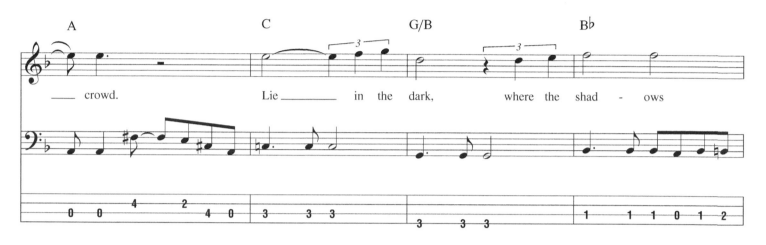

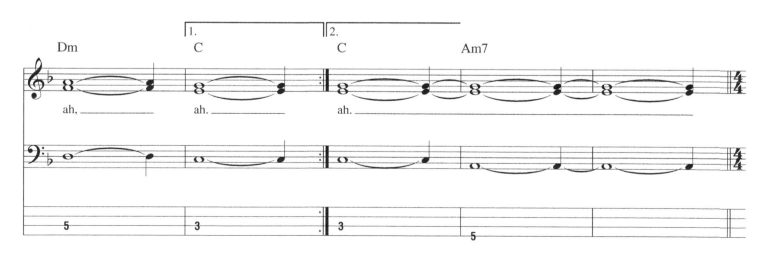

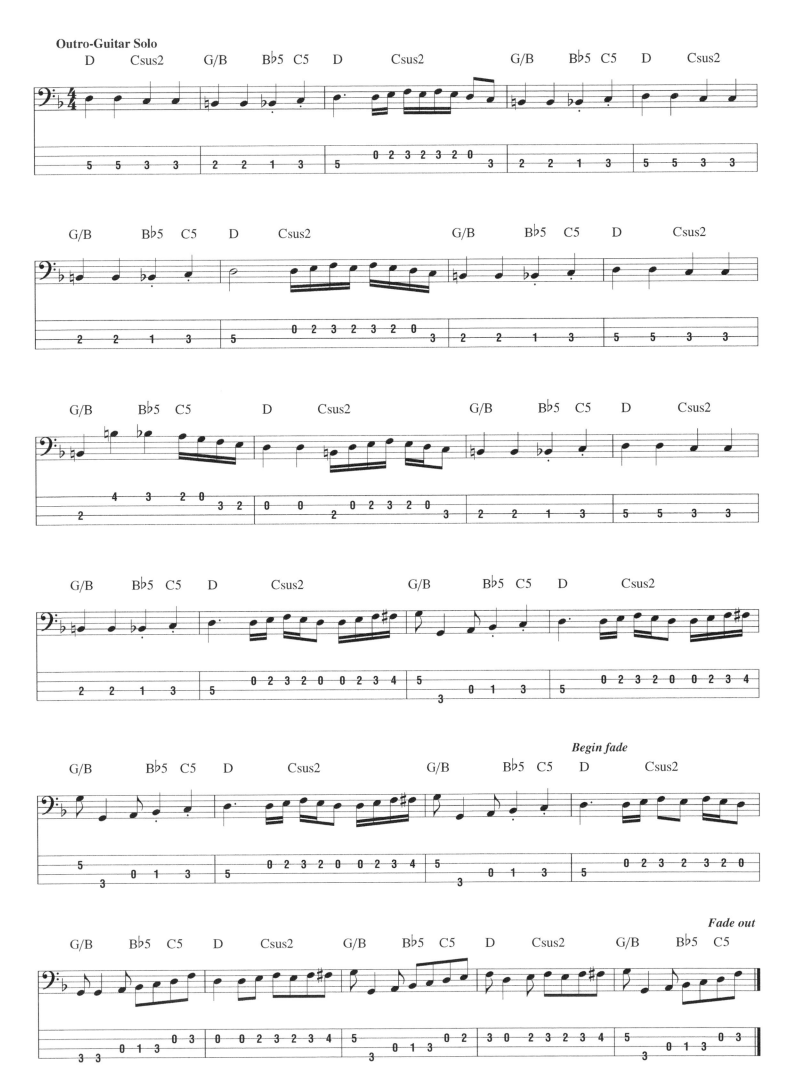

Werewolves of London

Words and Music by Warren Zevon, Robert Wachtel and LeRoy Marinel

Intro
Moderate Rock ♩ = 104

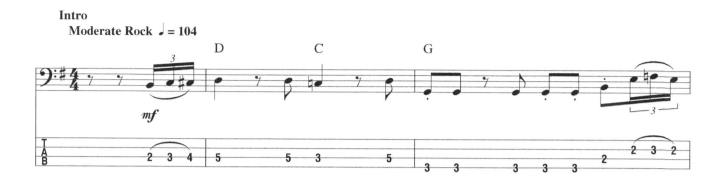

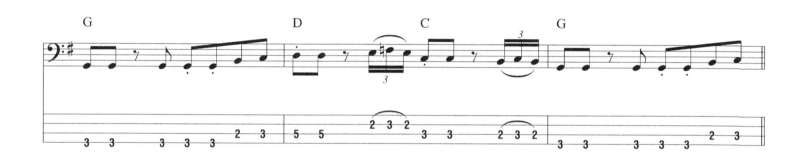

% Verse

1. I saw a were-wolf with a Chi-nese men-u in his hand __
2., 3. *See additional lyrics*

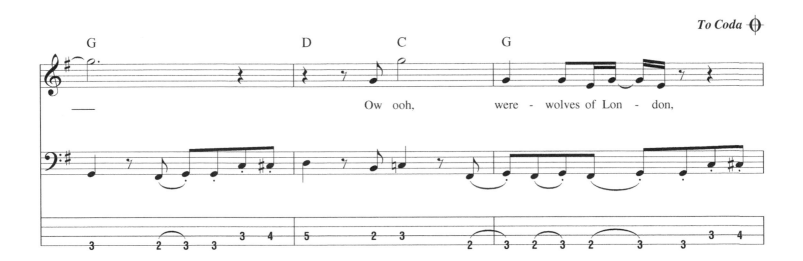

Ow ooh, were - wolves of Lon - don,

ow ooh. Huh!

Guitar Solo

D.S. al Coda

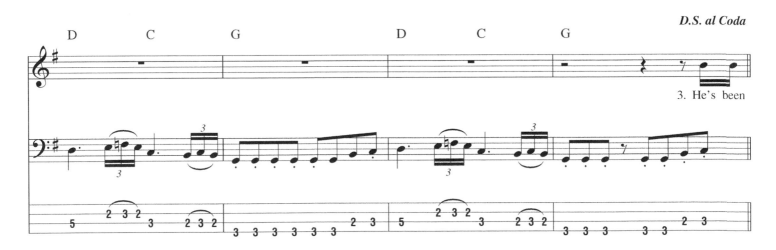

3. He's been

Coda

ow ooh. _____

Verse

4. I saw Lon Cha - ney walk - in' with the Queen _

do - in' the were - wolves _ of Lon - don.

I saw _ Lon Cha - ney jun - ior _ walk - in' with the Queen, _ uh,

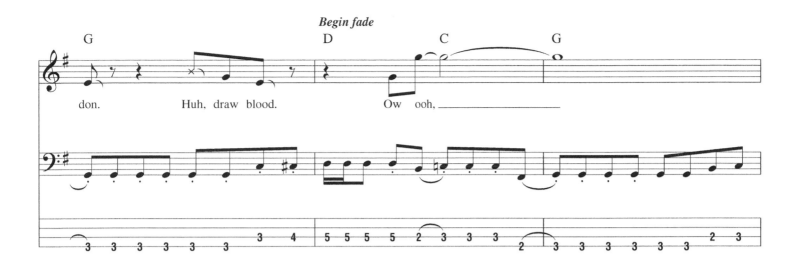

Additional Lyrics

2. You hear him howlin' around your kitchen door.
   You better not let him in.
   Little old lady got mutilated late last night.
   Werewolves of London again.

3. He's been a heavy handed gent who ran amuck in Kent.
   Lately he's been overheard in Mayfair.
   You better stay away from him, he'll rip your lungs out, Jim.
   Huh! I'd like to meet his tailor.

Won't Get Fooled Again

Words and Music by Pete Townshend

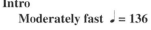

Intro

Moderately fast ♩ = 136

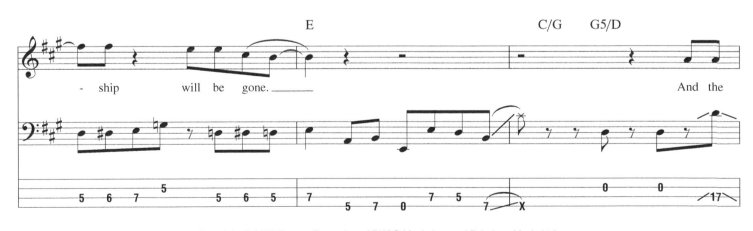

men who spurred us on ___ sit in judge-ment of all wrong, _ they de-

cide and the shot - gun sings the song. _ I'll

Chorus

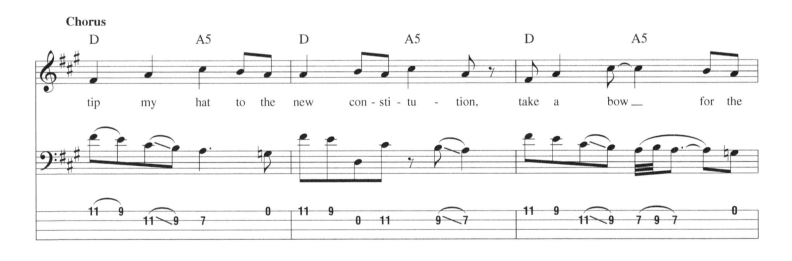

tip my hat to the new con-sti-tu - tion, take a bow _ for the

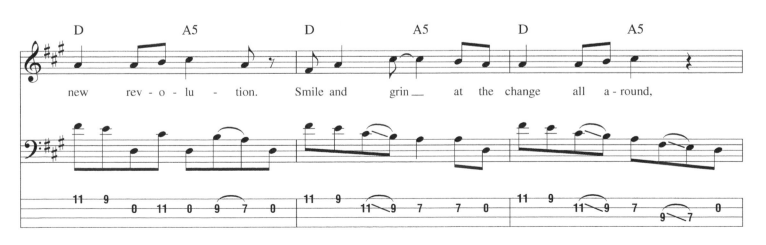

new rev - o - lu - tion. Smile and grin _ at the change all a-round,

pick up my gui-tar and play, ___ just like yes - ter-day, ___

___ then I'll get on my knees and pray ___

we don't get fooled _ a - gain. ___

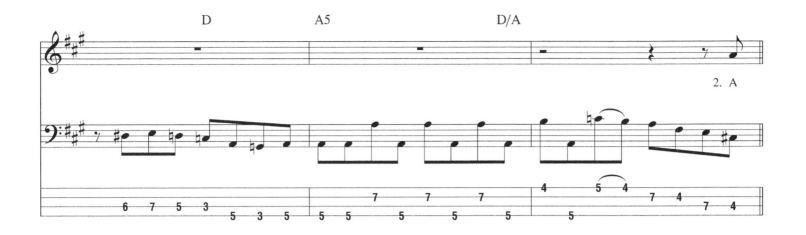

Verse

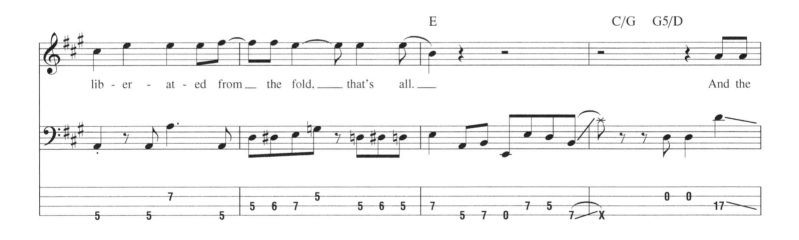

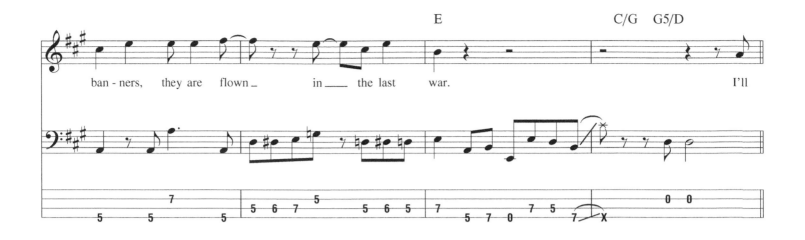

ban - ners, they are flown __ in __ the last war. I'll

Chorus

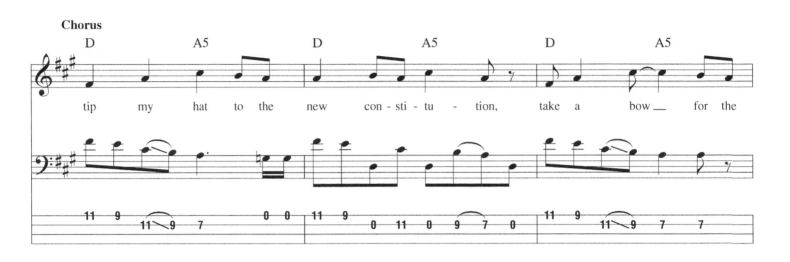

tip my hat to the new con - sti - tu - tion, take a bow __ for the

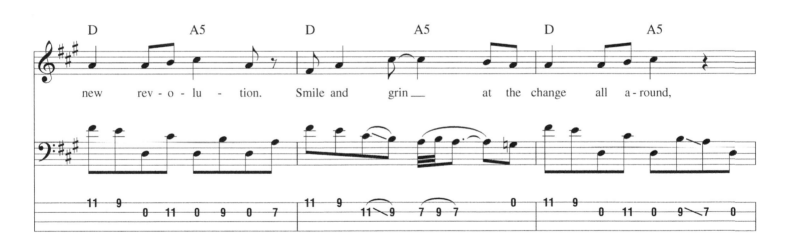

new rev - o - lu - tion. Smile and grin __ at the change all a - round,

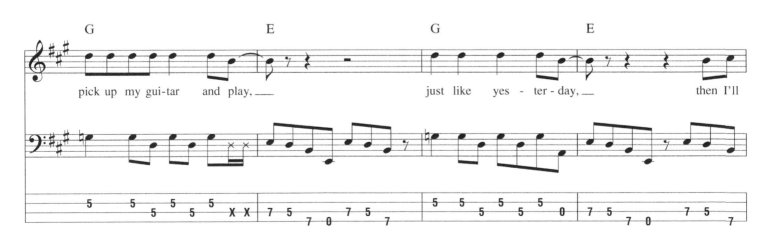

pick up my gui - tar and play, __ just like yes - ter - day, __ then I'll

get on my knees and pray

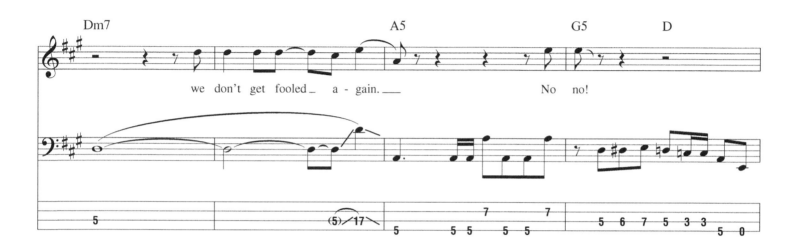

we don't get fooled — a - gain. ___ No no!

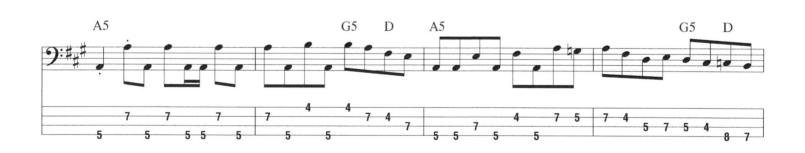

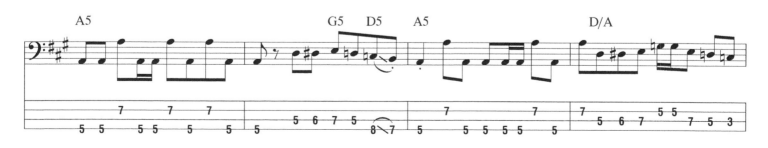

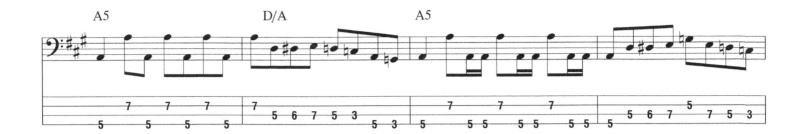

Bridge

I'll move my - self and my

fam - 'ly a - side, _____ if we hap - pen to be left half _____ a - live. _____ I'll

get all my pa - pers and smile _____ at the sky, oh, I know _____ that the hyp - no - tized

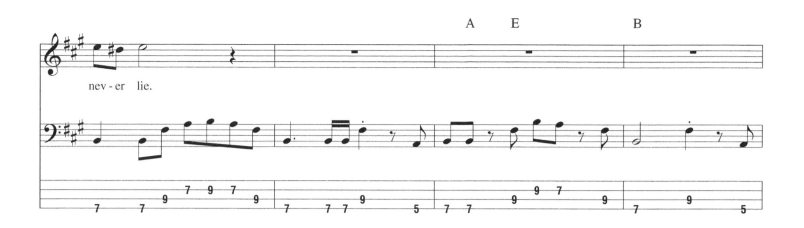

nev - er lie.

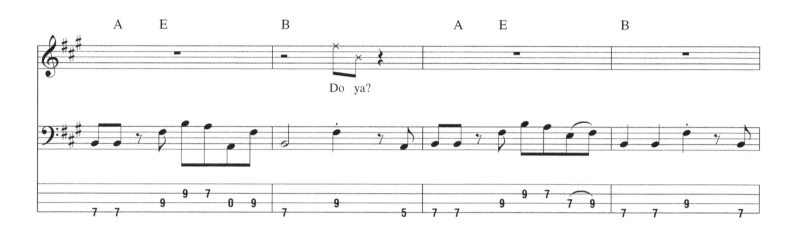

Do ya?

Guitar Solo

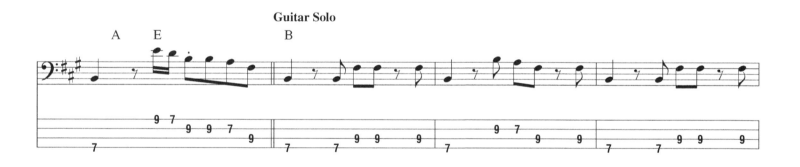

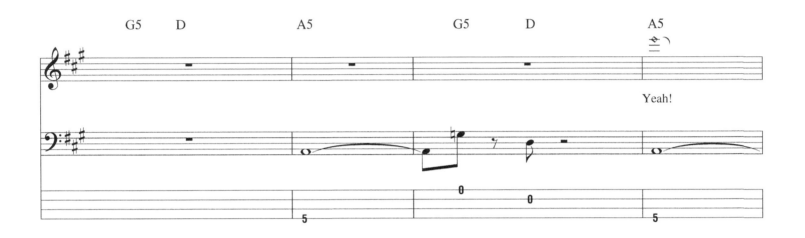

Yeah!

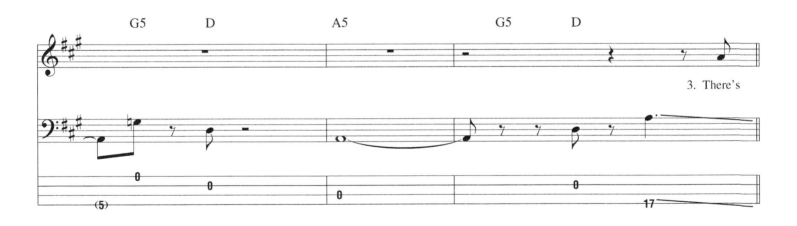

3. There's

Verse

noth-ing   in   the   street ___   looks an - y   dif - fer - ent   to   me, ___   and the

slo - gans are re - placed __ by __ the by. _____

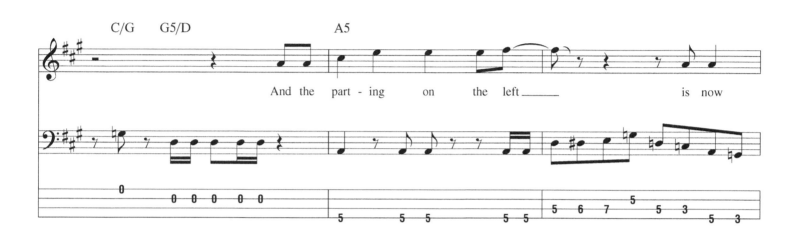

And the part - ing on the left _____ is now

part - ing on the right, __ and the beards have all __ grown long -

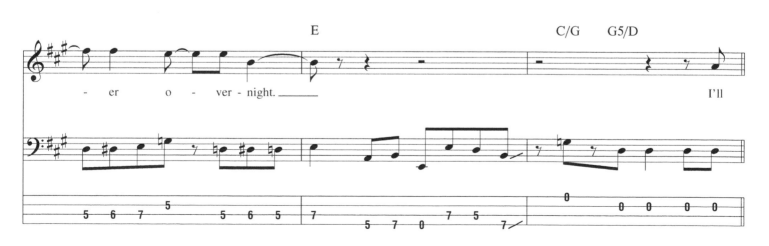

- er o - ver - night. _____ I'll

Chorus

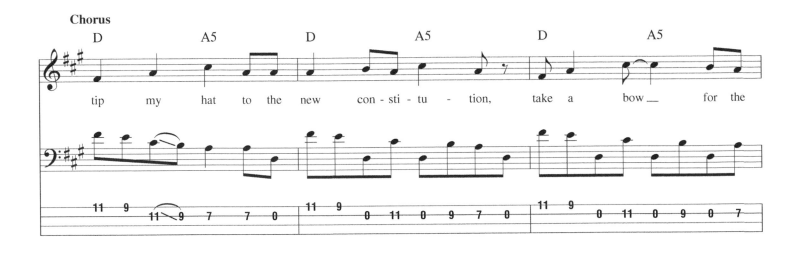

tip my hat to the new con - sti - tu - tion, take a bow __ for the

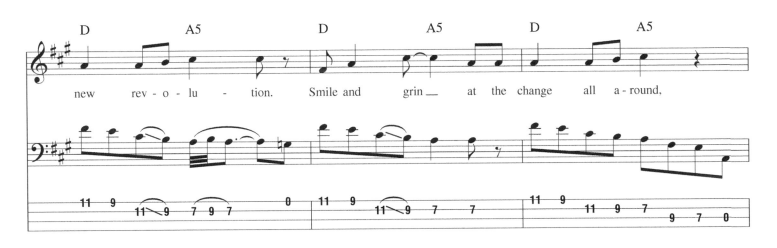

new rev - o - lu - tion. Smile and grin __ at the change all a - round,

pick up my gui - tar and play, ___ just like yes - ter - day, __

__ then I'll get on my knees and pray

we don't get fooled_ a - gain. _

Don't get fooled a - gain. _____ No, no!

N.C.(A)

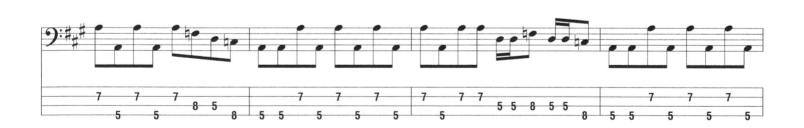

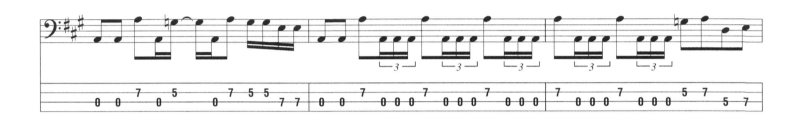

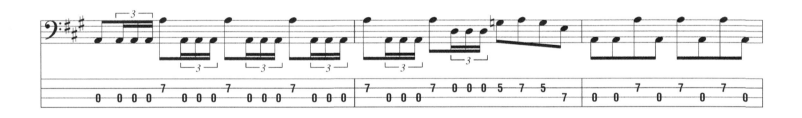

Interlude

A5

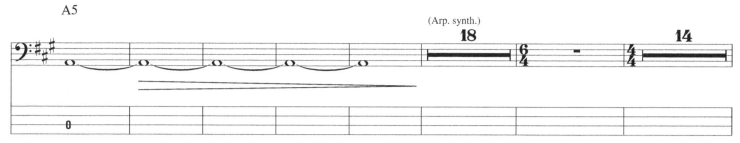

Outro

A5   G5   D   A5

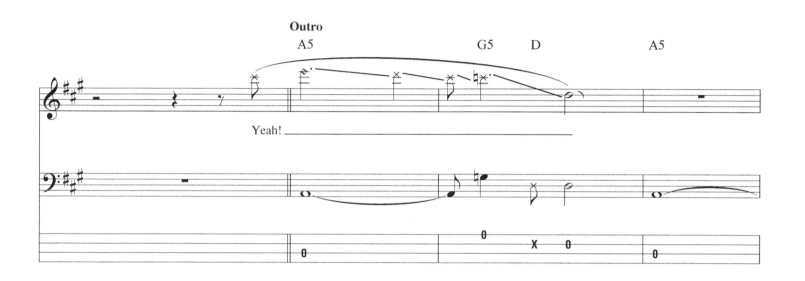

Yeah!

G5   D   A5   G5   D   A5

Meet   the   new   boss.   Same   as   the   old   boss.

G5   D   A5   G5   D

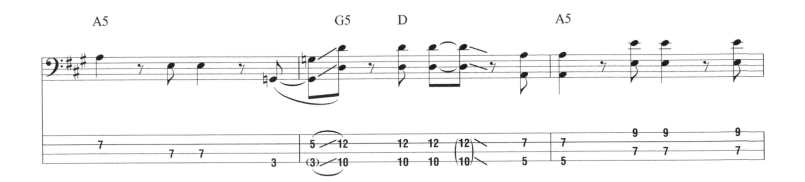

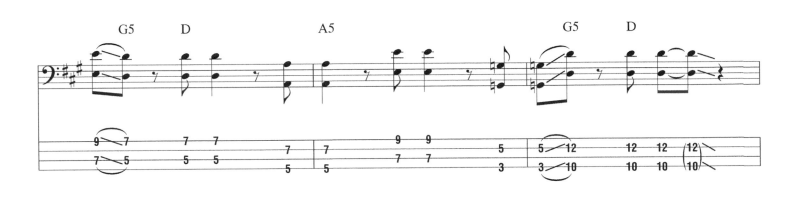

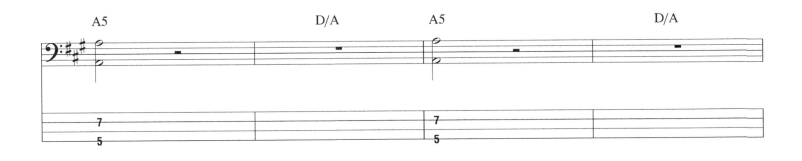

Free Time

(Townshend:) Hey! ___

Bass Notation Legend

Bass music can be notated two different ways: on a *musical staff*, and in *tablature*

Notes:

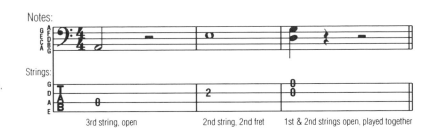

Strings:

3rd string, open   2nd string, 2nd fret   1st & 2nd strings open, played together

THE MUSICAL STAFF shows pitches and rhythms and is divided by bar lines into measures. Pitches are named after the first seven letters of the alphabet.

TABLATURE graphically represents the bass fingerboard. Each horizontal line represents a string, and each number represents a fret.

HAMMER-ON: Strike the first (lower) note with one finger, then sound the higher note (on the same string) with another finger by fretting it without picking.

PULL-OFF: Place both fingers on the notes to be sounded. Strike the first note and without picking, pull the finger off to sound the second (lower) note.

LEGATO SLIDE: Strike the first note and then slide the same fret-hand finger up or down to the second note. The second note is not struck.

SHIFT SLIDE: Same as legato slide, except the second note is struck.

TRILL: Very rapidly alternate between the notes indicated by continuously hammering on and pulling off.

TREMOLO PICKING: The note is picked as rapidly and continuously as possible.

VIBRATO: The string is vibrated by rapidly bending and releasing the note with the fretting hand.

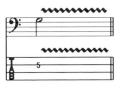

SHAKE: Using one finger, rapidly alternate between two notes on one string by sliding either a half-step above or below.

NATURAL HARMONIC: Strike the note while the fret hand lightly touches the string directly over the fret indicated.

MUFFLED STRINGS: A percussive sound is produced by laying the fret hand across the string(s) without depressing them and striking them with the pick hand.

BEND: Strike the note and bend up the interval shown.

BEND AND RELEASE: Strike the note and bend up as indicated, then release back to the original note. Only the first note is struck.

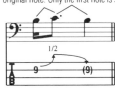

RIGHT-HAND TAP: Hammer ("tap") the fret indicated with the "pick-hand" index or middle finger and pull off to the note fretted by the fret hand.

LEFT-HAND TAP: Hammer ("tap") the fret indicated with the "fret-hand" index or middle finger.

SLAP: Strike ("slap") string with right-hand thumb.

POP: Snap ("pop") string with right-hand index or middle finger.

Additional Musical Definitions

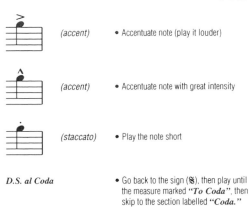

(accent) • Accentuate note (play it louder)

(accent) • Accentuate note with great intensity

(staccato) • Play the note short

D.S. al Coda • Go back to the sign (%), then play until the measure marked ***"To Coda"***, then skip to the section labelled ***"Coda."***

Fill • Label used to identify a brief pattern which is to be inserted into the arrangement.

• Repeat measures between signs.

• When a repeated section has different endings, play the first ending only the first time and the second ending only the second time.

HAL•LEONARD® BASS PLAY-ALONG

The Bass Play-Along™ Series will help you play your favorite songs quickly and easily! Just follow the tab, listen to the audio to hear how the bass should sound, and then play-along using the separate backing tracks. The melody and lyrics are also included in the book in case you want to sing, or to simply help you follow along. The audio files are enhanced so you can adjust the recording to any tempo without changing pitch!

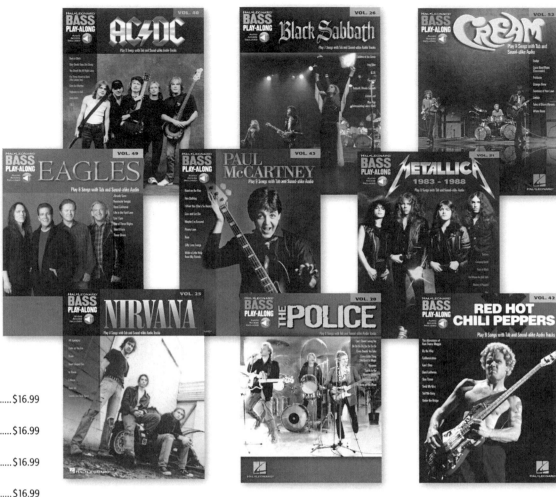

1. Rock
00699674 Book/Online Audio $16.99
2. R&B
00699675 Book/Online Audio $16.99
3. Songs for Beginners
00346426 Book/Online Audio $16.99
4. '90s Rock
00294992 Book/Online Audio $16.99
5. Funk
00699680 Book/Online Audio $16.99
6. Classic Rock
00699678 Book/Online Audio $17.99
8. Punk Rock
00699813 Book/CD Pack $12.95
9. Blues
00699817 Book/Online Audio $16.99
10. Jimi Hendrix – Smash Hits
00699815 Book/Online Audio.....................................$17.99
11. Country
00699818 Book/CD Pack $12.95
12. Punk Classics
00699814 Book/CD Pack $12.99
13. The Beatles
00275504 Book/Online Audio $17.99
14. Modern Rock
00699821 Book/CD Pack $14.99
15. Mainstream Rock
00699822 Book/CD Pack...$14.99
16. '80s Metal
00699825 Book/CD Pack...$16.99
17. Pop Metal
00699826 Book/CD Pack...$14.99
18. Blues Rock
00699828 Book/CD Pack...$19.99
19. Steely Dan
00700203 Book/Online Audio $17.99
20. The Police
00700270 Book/Online Audio $19.99
21. Metallica: 1983-1988
00234338 Book/Online Audio.....................................$19.99
22. Metallica: 1991-2016
00234339 Book/Online Audio.....................................$19.99

23. Pink Floyd – Dark Side of The Moon
00700847 Book/Online Audio $16.99
24. Weezer
00700960 Book/CD Pack..$17.99
25. Nirvana
00701047 Book/Online Audio $17.99
26. Black Sabbath
00701180 Book/Online Audio $17.99
27. Kiss
00701181 Book/Online Audio......................................$17.99
28. The Who
00701182 Book/Online Audio $19.99
29. Eric Clapton
00701183 Book/Online Audio $17.99
30. Early Rock
00701184 Book/CD Pack...$15.99
31. The 1970s
00701185 Book/CD Pack $14.99
32. Cover Band Hits
00211598 Book/Online Audio $16.99
33. Christmas Hits
00701197 Book/CD Pack..$12.99
34. Easy Songs
00701480 Book/Online Audio $17.99
35. Bob Marley
00701702 Book/Online Audio $17.99
36. Aerosmith
00701886 Book/CD Pack...$14.99
37. Modern Worship
00701920 Book/Online Audio......................................$19.99
38. Avenged Sevenfold
00702386 Book/CD Pack...$16.99
39. Queen
00702387 Book/Online Audio $17.99

40. AC/DC
14041594 Book/Online Audio......................................$17.99
41. U2
00702582 Book/Online Audio $19.99
42. Red Hot Chili Peppers
00702991 Book/Online Audio......................................$19.99
43. Paul McCartney
00703079 Book/Online Audio......................................$19.99
44. Megadeth
00703080 Book/CD Pack $16.99
45. Slipknot
00703201 Book/CD Pack $17.99
46. Best Bass Lines Ever
00103359 Book/Online Audio......................................$19.99
47. Dream Theater
00111940 Book/Online Audio $24.99
48. James Brown
00117421 Book/CD Pack...$16.99
49. Eagles
00119936 Book/Online Audio $17.99
50. Jaco Pastorius
00128407 Book/Online Audio......................................$17.99
51. Stevie Ray Vaughan
00146154 Book/CD Pack $16.99
52. Cream
00146159 Book/Online Audio......................................$19.99
56. Bob Seger
00275503 Book/Online Audio......................................$16.99
57. Iron Maiden
00278398 Book/Online Audio $17.99
58. Southern Rock
00278436 Book/Online Audio $17.99

HAL•LEONARD®

Visit Hal Leonard Online at **www.halleonard.com**